Smudge and Chewpen

A book of exercises for correction
of the common errors made in writing

Paul Groves and Nigel Grimshaw

Edward Arnold

© Paul Groves and Nigel Grimshaw 1976

First published 1976
by Edward Arnold (Publishers) Ltd
41 Bedford Square, London WC1B 3DQ

Edward Arnold (Australia) Pty Ltd
80 Waverley Road, Caulfield East
Victoria 3145, Australia

Reprinted 1977, 1978 (twice), 1979, 1980, 1981, 1982, 1984, 1986

ISBN: 0 7131 0090 7

Set 12/14 Photon Baskerville and printed
in Great Britain by Spottiswoode Ballantyne Ltd,
Colchester and London

Contents

1	Mixed capitals and small letters	1
2	Capitals for proper nouns	5
3	Sentence punctuation	9
4	Apostrophes for ownership	17
5	Apostrophes for missing letters	20
6	Spelling	22
7	To, too and two	24
8	Mixed errors	25
9	Speech punctuation	26
10	Play writing	34
11	Mixed errors	35
12	There, their and they're	37
13	Of and off	40
14	Should of, could of etc.	42
15	Spelling	44
16	Quite and quiet	46
17	Were and where	47
18	Was and were	48
19	Is, his, as, has	51
20	Letter layout and paragraphs	52
21	Mixed errors	59
22	No, now and know	60
23	Here and hear	62
24	Its and it's	63
25	Whose and who's	65
26	Your and you're	66
27	Mixed errors	67
28	Common spelling errors and tests	68
29	Revision and other exercises	72

To the teacher

This book is for those teachers who believe that accuracy in writing is an essential and a necessary part of the craft of communicating by writing. In our experience, however well the pupil is motivated to write he still makes many common errors which are constantly criticized by examiners and society in general. Indeed, very often the excitement of creative writing leads to a multitude of errors.

This book takes the commonest of those errors and deals with them in what we hope is a novel and humorous way. It takes them in the order in which they concern us. You may feel that they concern you in a different order. In that case, although the book reads like a story, the sections can be tackled independently. We have not dealt with specific problems caused by local dialect. If you have a particularly frequent error in your neighbourhood you may care to devise a 'Jim Smudge' type piece of writing to fit in with this book.

Virtually no grammatical terms are used and therefore certain generalizations have been used. We have also not dealt with errors which by their nature occur rarely in young people's work.

I Mixed capitals and small letters

Jim Smudge and Anne Chewpen are the worst children in Britain for making mistakes in their writing. This book is all about the terrible errors they make. We know that you are not as bad and will be able to spot all their mistakes, or at least most of them, and put them right. Just occasionally you may be making the same errors and this book will help you to put them right. Nobody writes without making mistakes. The printers of this book made some and we had to correct them before you saw the book. The thing is always to check your work before handing it in for the teacher to read. Sometimes we are excited by what we write or so relieved to have finished it that we hand it in straightaway. Jim and Anne do this all the time and you can see the result in this book. There are hundreds of errors made by them in the following pages. Jim's teacher, Mr R. E. Wright, thinks that Jim will be the cause of a shortage of red ink. Anne's teacher, Miss S. A. Madd, gets her red pens wholesale at the 'Cash and Carry'. How much red ink does your teacher use on your work?

One thing: although we want you to spot all the errors, **never write in or mark this book.**

Jim's big problem is his handwriting. It's not that you can't read it. Well, his teacher usually can, if Jim has not been in a hurry. It's the fact that he mixes up his small and capital letters. This is wrong. Most times we use small letters and we will show you this. Particularly bad are his b, d, p, r, and s. He writes them like this all the time:

B   D   P   R   S

So you get words like this:

PiPe   SeeS   PaRaDe   BaBy

In the Marion Richardson style of handwriting these are the capitals and the small letters:

Aa Bb Cc Dd Ee
Ff Gg Hh Ii Jj
Kk Ll Mm Nn Oo
Pp Qq Rr Ss Tt
Uu Vv Ww Xx Yy Zz

You may have a different style of handwriting. Check with your teacher that you are using the right small and capital letters for your style. Let your teacher know if you have a joining problem between letters. Do not use capitals unless you have been told to, as at the start of a sentence.

Here is some of Jim's work. We have had it typed out, as it might shock your teacher or perhaps ruin your eyesight. We want you to write it out in your books correctly.

Remember, do not try to correct this book or you will make a horrible mess.

```
One Day an olD tRamP waS going Down the RoaD.
He waS a veRy ScRuffy tRamP.  On hiS feet he
haD Some olD BootS with the SoleS coming off.
On hiS hanDS he haD Some mittenS with holeS in.
He waS weaRing a newSPaPeR foR a ShiRt.
```

If you corrected all the mistakes you would find 38. Did you correct them all?

Perhaps it wouldn't matter if Jim wrote only for himself; but other people see written work. One day Jim wrote to the Prime Minister. Old Wrighty started him off correctly with the address but then left him, and, oh dear!

```
DeaR PRime MiniSteR
I think it all wRong that School chilDRen woRk
for nothing.  I woRk veRy haRD at School and
So Do my mateS.  I am going to SuggeSt to you
that the GoveRnment ShoulD PaSS a law which
SayS that chilDRen ShoulD Be PaiD foR School
woRk.
YouRS faithfully.
Jim
PS  I Do homewoRk aS well anD that ShoulD Be
PaiD DouBle time.
```

We think you had better write this out correctly in your books. We will have more to say about letter writing later.

The Prime Minister was very shocked by Jim's handwriting. That very important person had just persuaded the Government to spend many millions of pounds on education. You can write the letter Jim might have received in reply when you get to page 72.

But before Jim had received a reply he had done some more work for Mr Wright. Here it is to correct:

```
I think the BeSt Day of the week iS SatuRDay.
When I have Done my PaPeR RounD I am free to
Do what I like.  I like to go Down town Best
with my mateS.  We go on ouR Bikes if one of
uS haS not got a PunctuRe.  FiRSt we get Some
Sweets anD then we have a gooD look RounD the
ShoPS.  I got a gooD kit laSt week of a GeRman
BomBeR.
```

There are two words here which are not the start of sentences yet correctly begin with capital letters. Did you spot them? More about these words, and others like them, when we meet Anne.

Next day Jim received his letter from the Prime Minister. He was so surprised that he decided to do something about it, especially as one of his ambitions was to be a Member of Parliament to represent all the school children of this country. His teacher asked him to write out this sentence as an exercise. It uses all the letters of the alphabet:

The quick brown fox jumps over the lazy dog.

Can you write this out correctly?

Note the small 'j'. Sometimes Jim uses the capital instead of the small 'j'.

He also got Jim to practise the letters he kept writing wrongly. He then got Jim to write out his favourite poem for handwriting practice. Here it is. You write it out too:

Ode to Egg and Chips

Oh egg and chips!
Oh egg and chips!

There's no such food doth grace the lips
As egg and chips.
Oh egg and chips!
Oh egg and chips!
Let's give three cheers and three hip hips
For egg and chips.
MP's dodge parliamentary whips
To stuff themselves with egg and chips.
And travel agents plan their trips
And plumbers mates ignore their drips
And swimmers leave their morning dips
And Chinamen their bamboo tips
With one accord to get to grips
With succulent plates of egg and chips.
Oh egg and chips!
Oh egg and chips!

Now copy out your favourite poem or a passage from a book
you enjoy.

2 Capitals for proper nouns

Anne Chewpen does not make the same mistake with capital
letters. 'Well done!' you might say. But no, she does not
bother to use capital letters at all. She writes everything in
small letters. You should start a word with a capital letter if it
is:

the start of a sentence

someone's name. (If you write your own name with capital letters, it is rude not to do the same with other people's.)

a day of the week or a month

something marked on a map like a town, a country, a river, a road, a mountain or a special building

a shop and the brand name of something sold in the shops

a title of your own work or other people's. (Stories, plays, poems, TV programmes.)

the letter *I* on its own

Look at this list and then correct Anne's work by writing it out in your books:

<u>best and worst</u>   <u>10th october</u>

i think that saturday is the worst day of the week. on saturday i have to do the cleaning and cooking and i cannot go out with my friend sally to northampstead. i think the best day is sunday because then i can lie in bed and eat a bar of cadbury's flake. i think january is the worst month in england because i get chilblains and i have to go to doctor gordon. i think august is the best month because we go to butlins at skegness. a lot of people in our road which is brompton road go as well. one year we went on the oxford canal and on the river thames in a boat and it was super.

How many missing capitals did you find here? You should have found more than thirty.

To help Anne, Miss Madd gave her this to copy out and in numbered sentences she had to explain why each word starting with a capital was written that way. You do it too:

Mrs Jane Tupley was walking down the High Street of Wellingfield one Tuesday in March. She was just passing Barclay's Bank when a strange man caught her eye. He looked like a Mexican or an Indian. He was reading the *Daily Mirror* but he kept glancing up. He looked frightened. Mrs Tupley was looking for the cheapest Heinz Beans she could find as her son, Gary, ate so many of them and she was on her way to Fine-Fare. Suddenly a car screeched out of Crompton Road . . .

Anne wrote:
1. Mrs Jane Tupley is someone's name.
You do the same for all the words starting with capital letters. Then finish the story and without being silly about it see how many words with capitals you can use in the story.

Anne improved after this but she would keep turning to talk to her friend Jayne and then she made a mistake. How many times has she made an error in the following piece of writing?

```
My ambition is to go and live in london.  I want
to work in one of the big shops like Selfridge's
in Oxford street and sell clothes.  when I am
old enough i will share a flat with my friend
Jayne.  We will live in chelsea near the King's
road.  at the week-ends we can go for walks by
the thames or if it is very cold we could stay
in and read a good book like 'Famous ghost
stories'.  i would buy boxes and boxes of after
eight mints.  for our holidays every August we
will go to spain and fly by british airways
from heathrow.
```

You write this out correctly.

When you have done this write out eight separate sentences which can be about anything but which must each contain one word using a capital letter apart from the word which begins the sentence. Look back at the list on pages 5 and 6. You might be clever and get several in one sentence.

Despite all this work Anne is finding this difficult because she will keep on talking to Jayne when she should be checking her work. Correct this piece and say what part of her work has improved:

There is not much to do in our town. There is the golden galleon which is a club in the watford road near to northampstead town hall. But it costs too much to go in there. There is the granada bingo club up near oak hill Park but that is for old people. There are several pubs like the White Lion near us and the cherry tree on the wimpey estate. I sometimes go to Watfield youth club or to the singing sands. The singing sands is a disco. Sometimes the Brandywine Band play at the youth club. They are a local pop group. I go dancing at the youth club quite a lot with my friend jayne.

3 Sentence punctuation

Jim was having a good time flicking paper pellets at Anne's neck which wasn't helping her with her capital letter problem. But Mr Wright caught him and told him to get on and finish his work or he would be kept in. So Jim rushed it. When Jim rushes or gets excited about his work this is what happens:

```
One night I was in a graveyard I don't know
how I got there I just woke up and I was there
it was very scary the moon was shining on the
tombstones all of a sudden I heard a creaking
sound it was like our larder door opening a
tombstone was moving and it had my name on the
top a skeleton got out of the grave but it had
my head on it my heart beat like a tom-tom I
tried to run but my leg caught in a creeper
then my Mum woke me up the sweat was pouring
off me
```

Yes, you've guessed. There's not a full-stop in sight. Although Anne can usually manage it, writing in sentences is probably one of the hardest things to learn in writing. But it is not so hard if you read your work through to yourself and see where you pause to make sense. Any piece of writing is a collection of sensible statements. You have to make sure that the people who read your work know when you want them to pause to get the sense right. Before you write out Jim's work correctly, read it through to see where he wanted the pauses.

Remember, a sentence is a unit of sense.

If you do not write in sentences you are often writing nonsense. (Did you sometimes have to puzzle over what Jim meant?) You might as well be writing in a foreign language.

Here is some more of Jim's work. We'll give you a clue about it. It is the start of an exciting story. This kind of writing often needs *short* sentences.

```
008 Jim Smudge looked up and down the street
he was a secret agent the street was very
quiet no one was watching him he went up to
the house there were no lights on anywhere in
the house he took out his knife carefully he
opened a window he climbed into a room it was
very dark Jim switched on his torch there was
a man tied to the chair it was Hamilton
Hamilton was another secret agent Jim spoke to
him Hamilton did not answer him Jim lifted up
his head there was blood on his face the man
was stone dead.
```

You should have found 19 sentences here. Did you?

Most writing mixes short and long sentences. Here is another piece of Jim's work to correct. Notice how *and* joins two sentences together:

```
It was a cold night moonlight shone like silver
on the sea I was walking along the shore I was
all alone suddenly I stopped out at sea I saw
a black object in the waves it came rapidly
closer I stood still watching it it was not a
```

```
boat but some strange shape at last I could
see what it was it was a head it had huge green
eyes it opened its mouth and its teeth were
huge with long points it saw me too and it
changed direction towards me I could not move
I was too afraid the sea monster came rapidly
nearer
```

Did you notice how *I* and *it* frequently start sentences?

The two *ands* Jim has used have joined up two short sentences into longer ones. This is one of the uses of this word. But it is a word we can over-use. We want to take you back to when Anne was younger. Just look at this!

```
when i have a nightmare it is always about
stairs and i am on stairs and they keep moving
like on the underground and a man chases me up
the stairs and i dodge out of the way at the
top and then i run down again and he still
chases me and I leap several stairs at a time
and in the end i find myself climbing up a
tower like blackpool tower and the man is still
there following me and i get to the top and i
am screaming and my mum wakes me up and tells
me not to mind and then she gets me a cup of tea
```

How many *ands* did you spot? Decide how many can be taken out to make new sentences instead. It is regarded as bad English to use too many *ands*. Also try reading this in one breath. At that time Anne had not been cured of her other problems so you had better correct those as well.

As you know Anne did improve but she caught the 'then' disease as Mr Wright calls it. In English, if you keep using the same word again and again it gets boring. Look what Anne has done here. Her mind wasn't really on her work as she was emptying her neighbour's bag for a joke and passing the contents round the class.

```
On some Saturdays I enjoy the day.  When I get
up I first get washed and dressed.  Then I go
down and have some breakfast.  Then after that
I go round and see Jayne.  Then we both go on
the bus down town.  Then we spend our time there
going round the shops then sometimes we buy a
record in the Play Inn.  Then at about twelve we
go home to have our dinner.  Then in the afternoon
we meet again at my house.  Then we play pop music
Then quite often we have our tea together.  Then
we go out at night sometimes.  Then usually we
go to a disco at the youthclub.  Then we spend
the evening dancing or talking to our friends.
Then when I go home I watch telly until I go to
bed.  Then on Sunday I do not do much because I
get up late.  Then I have my dinner at one.
Then if Jayne calls for me we go out for a walk
afterwards.
```

You had better correct this by taking out all the *thens* you think are unnecessary. Also write down what you think was Mr Wright's comment on this work.

Anne has a friend who instead of using 'then' all the time uses 'also'. This is just as bad. Check your work for this.

Mr Wright is always telling Jim that he is only 'half there'. He is not being rude; he is stating a fact. When Mr Wright was going on about sentences Jim seemed to be listening but he was actually seeing how close he could get the end of a thick felt pen to his friend's leg without actually touching him. As a result he got the idea that all you needed was some sort of mark to show where the sentences ended:

```
I do not like my Cousin Geoffrey, I think he is
a cissy, If we go out fishing he does not go
near the bank in case he falls in, he does not
like the maggots as well, sometimes I throw
them at him, he is always neat and tidy, and there
is not a single hole in his jeans, I do not think
he has been brought up properly, his parents are
always telling him not to do things, They will
not let him stay out after dark as well, When I
am a man I will bring my children up to be tough
like me, I will let them climb trees, and do
weight lifting, I will not mind how much dirt
they get on them.
```

Can you see that Jim has mistaken commas for full-stops?
Remember, a comma cannot do the work of a full-stop.
Rewrite this with capital letters and full-stops. There are two places where he has put a comma before *and*, where no punctuation is needed. Can you spot these two places?
Do not use a comma in a sentence until you can get your sentence punctuation right. Here is another piece of Jim's work to correct.

```
When I was younger there was a new building
```

site near us, I had a friend then, his name was
Dave, I used to call him Stew because he ate a
lot of stew, On Saturdays no one worked on the
building site, and you could get into the
houses. Stew and I went upstairs in one house
which was almost finished, There was a big
pile of sand outside the window and we had a
good time jumping in it, We played at spies,
and we knocked each other out of the window on
to the sand, when we got fed up with this we
played in a barrow that we found in a shed.
We gave each other rides in it, Stew found a
hose pipe with a narrow nozzle on the end, We
turned on the water, and played at putting out
fires in the houses, A man saw us and chased
us off. but he was old and we were too fast
for him, Stew got into trouble for getting wet,
My Dad blew me up as well, I remember that
Saturday and except for the end we had a grand
time.

Did you notice that once again he had put some unnecessary commas before the *ands*?

After this Jim got quite keen on full-stops. He made great
big ones; 'footballs' Mr Wright used to call them. The
trouble was that he put them sometimes where they were not
needed.

Remember, a sentence is a unit of sense.

You cannot mark off with a full-stop groups of words that
do not make sense.

Which of these make sense and are sentences and which are not sentences?

He was an old man
With a patch on his trousers
Because there were fourteen of them
John helped him
Which he did very often at the week-end
Keep off the grass
If I catch you on Thursday
When the mini-bus crashed there were three of our form in it
The four of them running down the road

Can you see that number of words or length has nothing to do with whether you have a sentence or not? You must ask yourself each time: 'Does it make sense?'

Take out Jim's footballs where they are not necessary so that this piece is written in proper sentences:

I am really quite good at English. Although I do
forget things. I think some parts of my brain
get crowded. Leaving no room for school work.
I remember when I was younger. That one day I
went to the shops for my Mum. I was talking to
Stew. Who is my mate. And we were kicking a
tin can along. When we reached the shop. I had
forgotten what I came for. I had to go all the
way back to our house. Which is on a hill.
Because I get up late some mornings. I come to
school without a tie. One teacher said that I
would forget my trousers one day. As I am so
forgetful. But I do not forget about mealtimes.

```
Or going to football matches.  I think that the
brain is a funny thing.  And I reckon I might
be a trick cyclist one day.
```

Here is a piece to punctuate which Miss Madd sometimes sets people like Jim and Anne because it contains the types of mistakes they make. You punctuate and also improve it in other ways.

```
slowly the fog came drifting over the town
the hills at first were hidden in it then
like a cat it crept into the dark streets
then it flowed out wider and wider covering
the roof-tops then in the early morning the
town woke up people walked slowly out of
their houses testing the ground with their
feet and there were no buses running and
like blind men and women they went along
the cloudy pavements and there were hardly
any sounds anywhere and there was only the
dull growl of a car or the mutter of voices
away in the fog
```

We have shown you a great deal of Jim's and Anne's work to do with sentences. But remember that it is no good correcting their work if you do not correct your own.

Remember, before handing in your work check the sentences.

4 Apostrophes for ownership

In his primary school Jim had learned about the apostrophe, that comma in the air. Only, while the teacher was talking about it, he was squirting water over Anne's legs from a plastic lemon. As a result he thought that you put an apostrophe before every *s* at the end of a word. Here is an example:

```
I like dog's.  I think that dog's are the best
pet's in the world.  When I am grown-up I am
going to have kennel's full of dog's.  I will
have Alsatian's and bull-dog's to guard my big
house and for dog show's.  I will keep Yorkshire
terrier's too to catch rat's.
```

Old Wrighty calls these apostrophes Jim's fly spots. He says it looks as though a dirty fly has crawled over Jim's paper. Yes, Jim has been wasting his time. None of these apostrophes was needed. Do you do that? If you do, even if it is only sometimes, write this out correctly. Then look at this paragraph. Two apostrophes have been used. Can you see any reason for them? If you cannot, remember this:

If you do not understand the apostrophe before an *s* do not use it at all. You will make far fewer mistakes this way. If you want to understand more about it read the rest of this section.

In English we talk about one as singular and more than one as plural. If you make a singular word like *dog* (one dog) into plural *dogs* (more than one dog), you do not have to use an apostrophe. This is where Jim goes wrong. This only happens when something is owned. If the dog owns a collar we write *dog's collar*. This shows us that one dog owns a collar. It is a shorter form of saying *the collar of the dog*.

You will find this ownership happening often with people's names:

Jim's book   Anne's pens   Mr Wright's laugh
Miss Madd's bad temper

See how the first word owns the second word or words. In each case we know there is only one person so it is not a normal plural. Now write these out correctly. Some of them will have apostrophes and some not:

dogs—cats—Jims knife—Annes trousers—slippers—houses—Mums best duster—spies—Dads old newspapers—elephants—matches—Grandads glasses.

When you have got them all right correct the following piece of Jim's work (note the apostrophe). He has not quite got it right yet. How many marks out of ten would you give him for this?

Mr Wright's lesson's are the best in the school. He is the best of all the teachers. He reads us storie's and thing's. Sometimes he reads us poems. I do not like them unless there are a lot of death's in them. Miss Madd's lessons are good as well. Her drama lessons are the best. She lets me and Gary Plinge be the crook's and then we have fights with the goodie's. Garys temper is terrible if he gets smashed on his glasse's. The worst lessons are Mr Oldens histor lessons. I mean to say who cares about Julius Caesar not being able to thread Cleopatra's needle? Also who is bothered about Henry the

Eighths ten wives and King John's jewel's being
lost in the laundry? What we should have are
demonstrations of karate or something useful
like how to keep boa-constrictor's.

Groaning to himself, Mr Wright pointed out all the
mistakes to Jim. How many was that? But Jim was watching
some men delivering coke outside. Has he done any better in
his next piece?

Mrs Barr's house is two door's down from ours.
Mrs Barr's front door is painted red and her
window's are white. In Mrs Barrs garden there
are a lot of flower's in summer. She always
has roses and lupin's and things like daisie's.
All we ever have in our garden are a lot of
dog's. Mrs Barr's husband is a little man.
We don't see him much as he is often at his
brothers house. But you can't miss Mrs Barr.
My Mum says she is like a dressmakers dummy as
she has so many clothe's. On the other side
of us but two house's away is Mrs Dawson. Mrs
Dawson's house is not as neat as Mrs Barrs
house. In fact it looks like the towns rubbish
tip. On the end of the row is a policemans
house. He always looks at me suspiciously as
though I have done a lot of crime's.

Write it out correctly.

**If after that you still do not understand the apostrophe
before an *s* do not use it at all and you will make far fewer
mistakes.**

5 Apostrophes for missing letters

Anne knows all about the apostrophe for owners. What she does not know about is the apostrophe for missing letters. Do you know what is wrong with this?

I did'nt like the way Jacky said it. She
should'nt have said it at all. It was'nt my
fault. It is'nt every day something like that
happens. I just could'nt believe it.

Yes, she has put all the apostrophes in the wrong place. They should be like this: didn't, shouldn't, wasn't, isn't, couldn't.

That is because the apostrophe shows a missing letter or letters. Do not put it where the words are joined but where the letter is missing. What letter is missing in the above examples?

Here is some more of Anne's work for you to write out correctly:

I did'nt want to tell you this. I would'nt want
it to get out and you must'nt tell a soul. I
really could'nt hold my head up again in Northampst
if I thought you had told. After all I do'nt want
to be thought a tell-tale. Well I have'nt got much
time and I ca'nt spend all day writing so I'll tell
you now. Mum thinks that Auntie Edna is going out
with the milkman. You know him from the Co-op with
the big moustache.

If you get into the habit of putting the apostrophe in the wrong place, it is a hard habit to break. So we think you had better correct one more piece of Anne's work. Anne is sometimes moody. Here is a piece she wrote after having an argument with Miss Madd one day:

There is'nt any need for schools. If teachers did'nt need jobs there would'nt be any schools. This country does'nt really need schools. If I did'nt have to go to school I would'nt be half so bored. I mean the world wo'nt come to an end just because I do'nt know about the apostrophe. My Mum says she does'nt understand it either. I ca'nt understand why I could'nt go out to work. I should'nt take any old job though. If I could'nt work for an airline I would train to be a hairdresser. We have'nt many hairdressers near here but I would'nt mind going into Northampstead or further to train. I should'nt think any work is as boring as school.

6 Spelling

We have been hiding from you the dreadfulness of Jim's spelling so as not to give you too much to correct. But at last Jim is going to do something about it as he wants to write a book on vampires. Mr Wright is going to give him one spelling to learn per day. Nothing upsets people more than bad spelling. Old army officers, clergymen and employers are always writing to the papers about people like Jim. If you have the same bother learn a word a day with Jim. Think of how many you will then be able to spell after one year. In case you have some of Jim's spelling problems, here is a piece of his early work to correct:

Until it realy happend I was not shure what to do at frist. I heared this niose comeing from the bushes. It was a big supprise. It was like somethink from a 'Doctor How' programe. Then I had an idear and I tryed hideing behind a tree but I surpose somethink was pokeing out. The nexted thing I new a big whip tentacle lashed out. I belive it was twenty feet long. It griped me like a boa-constrictor. I was cawt. The coulor was draining from my face and I was begining to loose conshusness. But I had not done my wieght training for nothink. With my bear hands I soon had it brocken in two.

How many of Jim's spellings did you have to correct? If he

had known the rule: **knock off the 'e' before 'ing'**, how many spellings would he not have got wrong?

Here is another Jim masterpiece:

```
Suddenley evryone was looking at the cieling.
To thier supprise blood was driping from the
lampshade.  008 dashed into the room above.
For a breif moment he could not beleive what
he saw.  The two spys were dead.  It was a
discusting site.  Flys buzzed round thier gory
bodys.  The cheif one had a label tied round
his neck.  It said THEIF!  The Blackgang bunch
had acheived thier aim.  He was overcome with
greif.  He sat down for a few minites.  Such
alot had happend since he got off the areoplane
and he felt allmost ready to give up.  He realy
did not have eny clues.  Then suddenley he had
an idear.  Quickley he thumbed threw his dairy
for the phone numbers.  As he saw the last
page he immediatley new what to do.  What a
releif.
```

Write this out correctly, please. Use a dictionary if you are not sure.

How many mistakes would Jim not have made if he had known the spelling rule: 'i' before 'e' except after 'c'?

What important exceptions to that rule are there in the two pieces of writing?

Note that English words end 'ly' and not 'ley'.

7 To, too and two

Anne has difficulty with *to, too* and *two* because she is *too* busy talking *to* her friend Jayne which she does every *two* minutes until Miss Madd gets cross. Do you have difficulty too?

Two is the easiest to learn; it just means the number 2.
Too is the hardest; it means more than enough as in *too* much or *too* small; it also means 'as well' as in he came *too*. If it has not got one of the above meanings it must be *to*. It is used in sentences like: He went *to* the pictures. It does not mean much *to* me. Do you have *to*?

See how many errors you can spot in this piece of Anne's work.

Yesterday I went to see my friend Tina. She wanted to see my new dress. I have too of them in the latest style. At first I thought they were to big and I thought I would have too go back to the shop but Mum said she would see to them on her new sewing machine. Marilyn was there to. She has been rude too me lately and I was not pleased to see her. I mean it was to bad of her to say to Tina I have no dress sense. I think she is too-faced. After all she wouldn't say that to me. It's not as if Marilyn has such marvellous dress sense herself. Her skirts are either to long or to short and

```
she sometimes comes to school looking like a
sack of potatoes.
```

Now write separate sentences using *to, too* or *two* in the order given below:

1	to . . . to	6	too . . . to
2	to . . . too	7	two . . . two
3	to . . . two		
4	two . . . to		
5	too . . . too		

Anne's writing is very gossipy. She never really tells us much. We are sure you can improve on it. Write a character description of Marilyn or the most tactless person you know. If you use to, too, or two underline them.

8 Mixed errors

Sometimes Anne seems to be getting a lot better at her work. At other times she just slips back into her old ways again. Miss Madd can get quite bad-tempered about it. On this particular day Anne had been told to write about her holidays but she was actually more concerned with a hole in her tights. How many errors can you spot?

```
next year when we go on holiday we sha'nt go to
mablethorpe.  we went last year in july and we
stayed at the Coppertree caravan park and we
```

```
did'nt have a very good time.  it was'nt that
the weather was to bad but my mum caught a
cold after too days and my dad wanted to take
her home but she would'nt go.  then my dad
caught the cold to and he was so ill that he
could'nt got out.  he did'nt get better till
we came home.  i wanted to go too skegness but
I could'nt.  i had to stay in the caravan and
look after mum and then we both had two look
after dad.
```

What do you think Miss Madd said about this?

Now write about your worst holiday and get your neighbour to check the English. Put in more detail about the place than Anne has given.

9 Speech punctuation

Both Jim and Anne like writing stories. Jim does, especially if there are plenty of deaths and a lot of blood spilt in them. The trouble is they often want to use speech. Here is a typical Jim effort:

```
The robot came forward "tell me your secret
code it said in a tinny voice "Never said 008
```

```
James Smudge "Tell me or I will exterminate you"
said the robot "if you do you will never find
the secret" said Jim I will torture you then
said the robot. A high-pitched whine came from
deep within it 008 clutched his head Ah! Give
in" cried the robot "No shouted 008 Tell no You
must Never I'll make it stronger you swine".
```

It's a mess, isn't it? Possibly you wondered at the end who was saying what.

The printers of books have a method of helping you with this. They set each new speech by the next person to speak on a fresh line. The first thing Jim must do is to learn to do this.

Don't worry about inverted commas and other punctuation until you have learned to do this.

Each new speech should be as follows and start with a capital letter:

The robot came forward. Tell me your secret code it said in a tinny voice.

Never said 008 James Smudge.

Tell me or I will exterminate you said the robot.

If you do you will never find the secret said Jim.

I will torture you then said the robot. A high-pitched whine came from deep within it.

Jim clutched his head. Ah!

Give in cried the robot.

No shouted Jim.

Tell.

No.

You must.

Never.

I'll make it stronger.

You swine.

See how much easier it is to read and how much more pleasant to look at. We also do not need a lot of 'said Jim' and 'said the robot' at the end because we can follow easily who is talking.

Note, too, how, if you want a sentence about the person who is speaking, it goes in the same section, like the one at the start of this piece of writing.

Now sort out some of Anne's work into speech sections. She is writing about an argument at the flats:

Mrs Jones knocked at the door of Mrs Williams's flat. Mrs Williams opened it. She had a fag stuck in her mouth "What do you want she asked. I've come about your television said Mrs Jones "What about it said Mrs Williams. Its too loud and it's keeping my Norman awake and he needs his sleep. "Are you suggesting we turn it off and don't watch it. We pay eight pounds a month for it said Mrs Williams "No just turn it down "What about your Kevin said Mrs Williams "What about him" asked Mrs Jones Why don't you turn him down" "Turn him down?" He shrieks and bawls outside this door like a maniac. "He's a nice quiet boy. He's always stamping up and down the steps like an elephant. Mrs Jones burst into tears. "You're the worst neighbour I've ever had she cried.

Now we are going to look back at Jim's work to put in the inverted commas and other punctuation. There are a few rules to follow and we give you the most important ones. Jim thinks this is a great deal of unnecessary fuss but he wants to get it right because he has just seen on TV a bloke who earned a million pounds writing a spy story.

1 All the actual words spoken should be enclosed in inverted commas at the beginning and at the end.

2 The punctuation before the 'said Jim' should be inside the inverted commas.

3 Each speech is a sentence even if it is only one word and it should begin with a capital letter and end with a comma, a full-stop, or other punctuation like a question mark or an exclamation mark.

The robot came forward. "Tell me your secret code," it said in a tinny voice.

1 Note the inverted commas.

2 Note the comma after 'code' is inside the final inverted commas.

3 Note the capital 'T' for 'Tell' and the full-stop after 'voice'.

The robot came forward. "Tell me your secret code," it said in a tinny voice.

"Never," said 008 James Smudge.

"Tell me or I will exterminate you," said the robot.

"If you do, you will never find the secret code," said Jim.

"I will torture you then," said the robot. A high-pitched whine came from deep within it.

Jim clutched his head. "Ah!"

"Give in!" cried the robot.

"No!" shouted Jim.

"Tell!"

"No!"

"You must!"

"Never!"

"I'll make it stronger!"

"You swine!"

1   Note that when the two characters shout or speak loudly the full-stop becomes an exclamation mark.

2   Note that like the comma the exclamation mark is inside the inverted commas.

3   Note that if you have not finished a sentence by the end of the page you go back to the margin. Look at the first and the fifth sections as an example of this.

4   Note that each speech is a new section.

If you are ever in doubt, look at a story book with speech in it. Check how the experts do it. The printers are very skilled at this. Sometimes they use single inverted commas but we think double are best for you.

One of the commonest mistakes in speech is to leave out the question mark. Speech often consists of question and answer. Did you notice that Anne has made this mistake? Sort hers out. We have started it here for you:

Mrs Jones knocked on the door of Mrs Williams's flat. Mrs Williams opened it. She had a fag stuck in her mouth. "What do you want?" she asked.

"I've come about the television," said Mrs Jones.

"What about it?" said Mrs Williams.

Note that the question marks are inside the inverted commas. Now complete this for Anne.

Jim started this off correctly. Then he started to watch a football match on the school field. Jim always sits by the window if he can. You had better set this out correctly for him:

```
Two old men were sitting on a bench.  "It's a
nice day," said the first.
        "You'll have to speak up I'm a bit deaf,"
said the second.
        "It's a nice day," repeated the first old
man.  "I don't think so, said the second.  Well
```

```
it may be a bit cold said the first.  It's very
cold said the second.  Perhaps said the first.
"In my young days the summers were really warm."
"Yes the summers were a lot better in the old
days.  "You could go out in your shirt sleeves.
"That's right you could and today look at all
the clothes you have to put on.
```

You may think it a bit odd for Jim to write about this but old Wrighty is mad about real dialogue, as he calls it, and this is a conversation Jim heard in the park.

There are two more points we would like to make about speech.

1   If you write more than one sentence in speech, provided that the sentence is not broken by a word like 'said' followed by the name of the speaker, you only need one pair of inverted commas at the beginning and one at the end:

"I want you to look at this work. I want you to look at it closely. It really is the most disgusting piece of writing I have ever seen. Rewrite it at once," said Mr Wright.

2   But, if a speech is ever broken, you need to open and close the speech commas again.

"I want you," said Mr Wright, "to look at this work again."

or

"I want you to look at this work," said Mr Wright. "I want you to look at it closely."

The first example in 2 is a single interrupted sentence.

The second example has two sentences split up by 'said Mr Wright'.

To give you more practice, here is an early piece of Jim's work:

The two cars screamed down the road. "They are
right on our tail shouted Hamilton. Leave it to
me " said 008 James Smudge. "I'll soon lose
them." "Watch that corner shouted Hamilton.
Sweat was beginning to ooze from his upper lip.
"I'll watch it said 008. The calmness of the
man was remarkable to see. "They're firing at
us." "Keep down shouted Hamilton. Get
your gun ordered 008 and fire back. Right said
Hamilton. Hold on tight said 008 I'm taking
this side road. Got him yelled Hamilton. I
got their tyre. They're swerving all over the
road. That will stop them said 008. It will
do more than stop them said Hamilton. They've
gone over that cliff.

And here is a piece of Anne's:

We went into the new house. "This is nice said
Mum. "It's a bit dark in the hall said Dad.
That's only the wallpaper", said Mum we can soon
change that. Let's have a look upstairs. "Three
bedrooms up here", said Dad they're too big.
"I like big rooms", said Mum. But there's that
blooming wallpaper again said Dad they must
have bought it by the lorry load. "Don't worry
about that said Mum wallpaper can soon be changed.
Not without spending a bit of money said Dad.
Come on said Mum let's have a look downstairs at

the other rooms and the kitchen I wonder who used to live here before said Dad. They had some wonderful ideas about wallpaper shut up about the wallpaper said Mum come downstairs. All right said Dad. This kitchen is a bit small said Mum and this cooker is very mucky never mind about that said Dad look at that garden that's a real garden that is. Do you like the house really asked Mum I can see that it's all right said Dad and anyway I'm not fussy. So we all went to live there.

When you have set this out in speech sections you may feel that some of the 'said Mum' 'said Dad' bits are unnecessary. If you do, cross some of them out.

Now have a conversation with your neighbour. Then write down what was said.

Then write some of these conversations:

in a doctor's or dentist's waiting room
at the hairdresser's salon
with an awkward customer in a shop
among the first group of people on the way to colonize the
    moon
between two mountaineers stuck on a rock face
between two drivers after a slight crash

Check! Check! Check! your speech punctuation.

10 Play writing

A word of warning

When you write out a play you do not need speech commas at all. Here is Jim's favourite joke of the week written out as a play:

Farmer Harry	My horse has got pneumonia.
Farmer George	Oh . . . Arh.
Farmer Harry	What did you give your horse when it had pneumonia?
Farmer George	I gave him paraffin.
Farmer Harry	Arh.

(One week later they meet again in the pub.)

Farmer Harry	Did you say you gave your horse paraffin?
Farmer George	Arh.
Farmer Harry	I gave it to mine and it died.
Farmer George	Arh. So did mine.

Note how there are no inverted commas at all. This means that play writing is easier than dialogue in a story.

Also note that, if you want to give any instructions to your actors or give other information, it is neat to put that well spaced in the text in brackets.

Now write out a conversation your family could have at breakfast like a play. It could begin like this:

Dad	It's cold this morning.
Mum	If you'd been up as long as I have, you wouldn't be.

Write out one of the conversations on page 33 in play form.

11 Mixed errors

Old Wrighty had read them something about animals. Now he wanted them to do some writing about animals they knew. This was right up Jim's street as he had just read a famous book about sharks. He began:

```
Dr Fang lived on a dessert island.  He kepted
man-eating sharks as pets.  Savige wolves garded
the place
```

"Smudge!" snapped Mr Wright. "I told you to write about animals you knew. I don't want one of your usual lurid stories."

"I don't know much about animals," said Jim. He had a good idea what lurid meant but he was not quite sure.

"You must have kept pets, lad," said Mr Wright. "You've got a dog too. And this time try not to make any spelling mistakes. Watch it!"

But Jim didn't watch it. He thought that writing about pets was babyish and paid little attention to what he was doing. It didn't please Mr Wright. There's no satisfying some people, is there? Can you see where Jim has gone wrong?

```
When I was just a little kid I kePt pet's,
we have a dog at home But last year we haD a
funny kind of Pet, my Dad was comeing home one
night when he stoped at the Back Door, he shouted
come here everybody.  we all went and looked,
it was a hedgehog in the dog's box.  Mum knew
```

what to Do I'll give it somethink she said
She put some milk in a saucer, the hedgehog eat
it and came evry night after that untill the
whether got colD, then it stoped comeing. We
all thought it was ~~hyb~~ ~~hyba~~ having a long winter
SleeP. There are lot's of story's about
hedgehog's, one say's that hedgehog's suck the
milk from a cow's teat, another say's that
hedgehog's can carry apple's on theiR Back's
stuck in the spine's. In my Dreams I sometimes
imagin that a big hedgehog gets in my bed, it
lifts up the sheets and the cold gets in then
it Rubs itsself down my back and its huge spines
Stick in me I look up and see one of its big
eyes looking into mine. I think that would make
a good TV program the world coulD be invaded by
giant hegdehogs whose spines were so thick you
couldn't shoot them

Although he was cross about the errors, there was one part
of this writing which Mr Wright liked and another part he
didn't think much of at all. What do you feel about it as a
piece of writing?

With the help of an encyclopedia, write about some
animal, like an elephant, that has mythical stories about it.
Concentrate on the facts but decide whether you would like
to put any other information in.

Then check your work for the kind of errors Jim makes.

12 There, their and they're

Jim has problems with: there, their and they're. It's because they're (they are) all pronounced the same. He thinks old Wrighty is making a fuss about nothing. What does it matter if he gets a few wrong? But with Jim it's not a few and it happens in almost every piece of work that he does.

Note   'There' is the place word like: 'There he is, over there'. It is also the word that comes before: is, are, was, were. It is often found at the beginning of a sentence.

Note   'Their' is the owner word. It shows possession as in: their books, their houses, their manners, their bus.

Note   'They're' is the hardest to spot. It is an abbreviation for 'they are'. You find it most in speech.

Note   If you are not sure, check whether it is the possessive 'their' or the abbreviation 'they're'. If it does not seem to be either of these two it must be 'there'.

Jim was very proud of this work because he knew he had set out the speech correctly. But Mr Wright was not so pleased. Can you see why? If you can, write it out correctly.

```
        "There over their," said the cop.
        "There not.  You can tell by there car,"
  said 008.  Their was a look of determination in
  his eyes.  "I can also see there footprints in
  the mud over there," he added.
  Their were now a load of cops their but they
  obviously had there hands full with the Blackgang
  bunch.  They had had them cornered before but
```

to their surprise they had escaped. But this
time OO8 was at they're side.

    "I think their going to break cover," he
said.
Sure enough there black masked heads could
suddenly be seen popping up over the sea wall.
The police fired but there aim was no good.

    "Leave them to me, their mine," said OO8.
There was no doubting the accuracy of his aim.
There death was quick. Each of the six bullets
hit one of there masked heads.

If you did this correctly, you should have found sixteen
errors. Did you? If not, look again. If you did spot sixteen
errors, did you make the right correction? Look back again
at the explanation at the start of this section.

One day Mr Wright set the class to write about a football
match. Jim rather fancies himself as an ace reporter and as
well as working for MI5 he thinks he will cover the big
matches as well for the *Sunday People*.

There was a big crowd at Northampstead United's
ground. It was there last game and it was
they're most important match of the season.
All their championship hopes rested on there
performance in this match. There supporters
cheered as they ran out onto the park. The
team looked good in they're blue and white strip
Then the cheering and singing stopped.

    "Where's their eleventh man?" someone
shouted. "Their a man short."

Jim looked down at the manager's bench. The manager held his head in his hands. The rumour went round the crowd. There star player had slipped on a piece of orange peel coming out of the dressing room and broken his leg and the substitutes had suddenly caught the flu. It looked as if United would lose there last game. Jim leaped over the crowd and suddenly there he was telling the manager not to worry. He would get them out of their difficulties. Quickly he changed. The crowd started there cheering and singing again.

"What on earth are you doing, Smudge?" asked Mr Wright. "I asked you to write about a real football match. Let me just check this for *there, their* and *they're* before you begin again." What did he find?

Now write separate sentences using *there, their* and *they're* in the order given.

1 there ... there
2 there ... their
3 there ... they're
4 their ... their
5 their ... there
6 their ... they're
7 they're ... there
8 they're ... their
9 they're ... they're
10 Try and get all three words in a sentence in any order

13 Of and off

Anne will day-dream about her latest pop star idol. When she does she often mixes up *of* and *off*. This is simply put right by asking yourself whether you mean *of* pronounced *ov* or *off* pronounced with an *f* sound. You have a lot *of* (ov) homework to do but you get *off* a bus. Most people can spot this mistake when it is pointed out to them. So what is needed again is careful checking. Check this piece *of* Anne's and write it out correctly:

```
I have got a lot off records.  On Saturday I
usually get some money of my Dad and then go off
down town.  I get of the bus at Woolies.  I
nearly always buy the record which is 'Top off
the Pops' and one more.  Off course if I don't
like the record at the top of the charts or if
I have got it I buy two of those I like the best.
One day I knocked a big pile of the shelf.  The
woman wasn't half mad.  I reckon she could have
knocked my head of.  I reckon it was mean of
her to shout at me though.  Of course I didn't
mean to knock them of.  Then all of a sudden
this boy with lots of black hair was there helping
me to pick all of them up.
        "I knocked them of last week," he said.
"Off all the stupid places to keep them."
```

```
This got the woman really mad.  "Clear of the
pair of you," she said.  "I get too many off
your sort in here on Saturday."
Well this boy got the manager.  I wouldn't have
dared.  "Can I be of assistance to you?" he said
ever so posh.  This boy told him all about what
had happened and then as we left the shop we
could see him telling her of.
```

Now write separate sentences using *of* and *off* in the order given:

1 of . . . of
2 of . . . off
3 off . . . of
4 off . . . off

We think that Anne's experience in Woolworth's would have been more interesting if she had put in more details about the sights, sounds and smells of Woolworth's on a crowded Saturday. See if you can write a better piece. If you use *of* or *off* underline it.

14 Should of, could of etc.

Jim just doesn't day-dream; he drops right *off*. One day, after watching a late night horror film, he slept for ten minutes while Mr Wright was reading from *The Invisible Man*. He was dreaming that he couldn't be seen.

Jim has an *of* problem too. What he does is to write *of* for *have* after these words: should, could, would, might, must and may. If we are honest most of us say 'couldov' and not 'could have'.

Learn this and you will get it right.
Never write 'of' after should, could, would, might, must and may.

It should always be:

should have
could have
would have
might have
must have
may have

You can see this problem in the piece of extra work Jim had to do for old Wrighty after school about invisibility. We think you had better write it out correctly:

```
I could of screamed when I saw the invisible
monster's foot-prints.  I would of done if I
hadn't dug my nails into my rifle butt till my
fingers bled.  I realised I should of shot it
when I had the anti-monster rockets.  I could
```

of done easily and it would of sunk in the
slime of the swamp. Now I only had my automatic
rifle. I could of cried. I should of left
nothing to chance. I would of been acclaimed
as a hero as I might of saved the town below
from the ravages of the invisible man-eater.
I must of been the biggest fool in the world.
I might easily of been killed.

Jim then got tired of this and there was still some time to
go. So he wrote this:

Jim could of escaped from the prison camp alone.
But he would of left Steve in the camp. They
were both outside the hut. The light moved
round and if they hadn't ducked the guards must
of seen them. They ran forward. Then the light
probed again. Jim threw himself flat. Steve
should of dropped to the ground as well. But
he must of been too slow. The light caught
him. Jim could of run for it and reached the
wire safely. A shot rang out. Steve fell. He
must of been badly wounded. Otherwise he would
not of groaned so. Three guards ran at them.
Three should of been enough but Jim had done
weight-training and karate. He knocked all three
out. Carrying Steve he ran to the wire. Jim
could not tell in the dark but Steve might of been
wounded in the shoulder. He could of left

```
Steve then and saved himself.  But with Steve
over his other shoulder he ran off into the
night.
```

You had better write this out correctly. Did you spot the one 'of' separated by the word 'not'? What do you think Mr Wright did to Jim after this? Do not be too hard on him because you have probably had this mistake marked in your book. Watch out for it!

Now write separate sentences using each of the following words:

1 ... should have ...	7 ... should not have ...
2 ... could have ...	8 ... could not have ...
3 ... would have ...	9 ... would not have ...
4 ... might have ...	10 ... might not have ...
5 ... must have ...	11 ... must not have ...
6 ... may have ...	12 ... may not have ...

15 Spelling

Miss Madd is potty about creative writing. She has not had much success yet with Jim. When she asked him to write about autumn, Jim's essay began: 'From the rusty brown leaves in Warlock's Wood a leg stuck out . . .' You can probably guess the rest. She really lived up to her name when, after she had spent ages talking about rain and reading the class poems, Jim's writing began; 'There was a rain of bullets as 008 ducked . . .'

She has had more success with Anne. But, as with Jim, we have not mentioned that Anne's spelling is not all that brilliant. If you can spot any spelling mistakes in this you had better write them out correctly:

```
Of all the diffrent kinds of whether I like
summer rain more than anythink.  I mean the
soft kind that comes in a shower on a hot day.
Unfortunatley we do not seam to get alot and
that seams to keep comeing at night.  What I
like about it is the smell.  When the clouds
have dissapeared and the sun is shinning
agian you can go out and walk on the clean
pavments.  The sun is warm on your neck and
there is a feeling like being under an electric
blankit.  The smell is hard to discribe but it
reminds me of a soap Mum buys at Christmas.  I
want to put on chiffon old-fashiond cloths and
dance slowly and effortlessley like in a TV
advertisment.  I do not mean thunderstorms
with lightening.  I am frightend of them and
so are most of my freinds.  I then think of
the angrey Greek gods hurling down thunderbolts.
```

If you turn to pages 68 and 69 you will find a list of the spellings Jim and Anne have most frequently got wrong during their school career. How many on this list do you get wrong? If there are several, think about joining Jim and learning one a day.

16 Quite and quiet

Quite and *quiet* give Jim a lot of bother. They shouldn't because they are pronounced differently. Here is a piece of his work to correct. Ask yourself which word he means and say it over in your mind every time you come to a *quite* or a *quiet*. Remember that *quiet* means silence. Here is Jim writing down as a punishment what Mr Wright said:

```
"I want you to keep quiet quite," said Mr
Wright.  "We have had quiet enough nonsense
this morning.  When I say quite I mean quite.
I want no shuffling or pencils tapping on the
desk.  I am quiet sure the headmaster would be
very annoyed at the work you have done.  It is
quite disgusting.  You keep quite.  Stop
fidgeting.  I want you as quiet as a church
mouse.  In fact I am quiet disgusted with your
work all this week.  I suppose it's because I
told you it was quiet good last week and now
you have stopped concentrating.  Jim Smudge,
if you cannot keep quiet you will have to
write out what I am saying.  It is quiet
ridiculous if a boy of your age cannot keep
quite still."
```

And Jim had to. This is his first effort. He had to do it twice before he got it right. How many times will you have to do it?

Now write separate sentences using *quite* and *quiet* in the order given:

1 quite . . . quite
2 quite . . . quiet
3 quiet . . . quiet
4 quiet . . . quite

17 Were and where

Two other words that get Jim into a fog are *where* and *were*.
You use *where* when you are talking about a place: "*Where* is
the railway station?" (In what place is the railway station?) or
"I don't know *where* to find him." (I don't know in which
place to find him.)

Were is often used when talking about some kind of action:
The supporters *were* singing. They *were* coming home.

These words are pronounced differently. Train your ear to
listen for the difference in the sound.

Can you see *where* he has gone wrong in this? Do you think
they *were* bad mistakes?

```
008 nodded at Hamilton and looked out of the
railway van.  Were where they?  There where
fields all round and how many of the enemy were
hidden in those tall hedges?  Where they coming
to a station?  He looked down the track risking
```

a bullet in the head. There were buildings
down there. He could see were the track went
round a bend past the spot where the buildings
where. How many of them were hidden in there?
The train was slowing down. Soon he would
know exactly were they where. When they
arrived where they wanted to be the danger would
begin. There where things he and Hamilton
wanted to do. Were where the explosives? Silly
as it seemed he had forgotten where he had
hidden them. They had better find where they
where quick.

Now write separate sentences using *where* and *were* in the
order given:

1 where . . . where
2 where . . . were
3 were . . . were
4 were . . . where

18 Was and were

Both Jim and Anne sometimes write *was* for *were*. This is a
fairly difficult habit to get out of in writing as it is frequently
part of a local dialect in some areas. Normally if we are

writing about one person we use *was*, except with the word 'you': I *was* there; you *were* there; he, she or it *was* there. If we are talking about more than one person we use *were* normally: we *were* there; you *were* there; they *were* there. This table may help:

Singular	Plural
I was	we were
you were	you were
he, she, it was	they were

Here are some more examples:

Singular	The striker *was* playing well.
Plural	The players *were* soon exhausted.
Singular	The goalkeeper *wasn't* on form.
Plural	The linesmen *weren't* going to be fooled.
Singular	There *was* only one goal scored.
Plural	There *were* five goals in the first half.
Singular	*Was* it the state of the pitch?
Plural	*Were* they going to lose?

A further complication is that when you have a singular word meaning 'many' or 'several' like the word 'team' you can say either: 'The team *was* doing well' or 'The team *were* doing well' depending on whether you are thinking of the team as a unit or as several different players.

There are more things to learn about *was* and *were* but this is plenty to be going on with.

In the following piece of writing Jim has used *was* every time. When should it have been *were*?

```
    "You was there," he said.
    "No, I wasn't," Jim said, "nor was the
others.  We was never there at all."
    "Yes you was."
    "No, we wasn't.  They was but we wasn't."
```

The policeman stopped smiling. "I think you was all there together. There was six of you."

"No, the Suez Street gang was there but my friends wasn't."

"If you are sensible you'll tell the truth," said the policeman.

"I wasn't there. Gary wasn't either. We wasn't there at all."

"I think you was all there," repeated the policeman. He was clearly losing his patience. The Suez Street gang was there, you was there, and your five friends was there." He brought out a photograph.

Jim looked at it. He did not know what to do now. Was it right to go on protecting Gary? Another two boys was being brought into the room. Were they from the Suez Street gang? Three policemen was with them. He could see now he was in for it.

Another complication is that where a writer wants to use a local dialect form as in, say, *Coronation Street* it is quite correct to use English which in writing is regarded as incorrect if that is how the writer wants the character to speak. For example 'us' is frequently used by the characters for the word 'our'. In the passage you have just corrected it could be argued that if that was the way Jim spoke it would be correct. But what about the policeman?

19 Is, his, as, has

Another problem connected with dialect is the tendency of people to leave off aitches in some areas of the country. This creates problems in writing with *is* and *his*, and *as* and *has*.

His is the ownership word: *his* boots, *his* temper etc.

As and *has* are harder to understand. We frequently use *as* to mean 'while' or 'because'. We also use it in expressions like 'as if' and in comparisons like 'as big as'. Note that it is always 'He has' and 'She has' and 'It has'. To tell you more about *has* might leave you muddled. The best way of learning the difference between these two words is to listen to newscasters on the TV. They talk a kind of standard English called Received Pronunciation in which all aitches are put on.

A friend of Jim's always writes *is* and *as*. See how you get on correcting his work.

```
As I am going to the fair I see my friend.  He
as a bicycle that as a broken saddle on it.
As he rides he can hardly sit on the saddle as
it is in two pieces.

    "You'll fall off one day", I say.
He as a funny sense of humour.  "Only to pick
up a pound note," he says.  Is face jerks up
as if it was built on springs and he as this
explosion of a laugh which as us falling about
at school.

    "As the fair started yet?" I ask.
```

"I'm fairly sure it as," he says with a grin as if is head would split in two.

"I can't wait to get my teeth into a hot dog," I tell him.

"Just stick a match under that Alsatian then," he says. He has teeth as big as a horse's. They almost seem to split is lips. He rides off round the corner as if he as been chased by a bull.

Suddenly there is a crash. As he come off?

I run round the corner. He is sitting on the ground with a tyre round is neck as if it is a snake. He yawns as if he was going to swallow is hand. "Gosh, I'm tired," he says.

20 Letter layout and paragraphs

Anne likes writing letters, but she goes wrong from the start. After poor spelling nothing seems to annoy people more than badly written or set out letters. In a way a letter is like an advert: it advertises you as a person. You can tell a great deal about a person by the way he or she writes a letter. Here is the start of a letter by Anne:

93 Colne rd

Watfield

   northampstead

Herts

Monday

Can you see what she has done? Yes, she has forgotten her capital letter rules. Each word in the address should begin with a capital letter. She could also line it up better as well. Most people slope the address from right to left. Here it is correctly done:

93 Colne Road

Watfield

   Northampstead

Herts

HN32 1BD

8 November 1976

Note that we have written 'Road' for 'rd'. It is common these days to write 'Road' or 'Street' etc. in full. It is also modern practice to leave out the punctuation in addresses. This is lucky for you, as it makes it a great deal easier. Note, as well, the date. The correct date is more accurate than 'Monday'. It has also now become important to put in the postal code.

Now write out your address correctly. Remember, if you start a letter correctly, you are more likely to take care with the rest of it.

Here is one of Anne's letters after the heading:

Dear Carole

Thank you for your letter. it was
ever so nice to hear about the things you
had done on the school trip to france.
My holiday was not half so exciting as
yours. i went to Skegness again with
my parents and my horrible little brother.
Do you know he put a crab down my back
and I can't stand creepy crawly things.
We stayed in a caravan at ingoldmells.
it was very modern and it had a shower in
it. i shall buy one one day when I am
married and have holidays every week-end.
On the first day we went into skegness in
the car and went to the fun fair. my brother
went on everythink but i dared only go on
the galloping horses and the dodgems. There
were some funny mirrows there in the fun
house. i have never heard my Mum laugh so
much. For the next four days it was so fine
we lay on the beach. That was when I got
the crab down my back. Mum went too bingo
alot and won a lovely big teddy which she
gave to me. I think my brother was jealus
about this. on the last day we went on the
boating lake which was good fun as I did
not have to row in the evening there was a
big display of fireworks. We drove home

through the illuminations. There was a
full moon and it looked ever so romantic
so much better than grotty northampstead.

See you soon

Love

Anne xxxxx

This is a very pleasant letter from Anne but it is all written in a block. It is not very attractive to the eye. To help the reader writing is set out in paragraphs. You put together things on the same theme into a paragraph. There should be four paragraphs in Anne's letter.

The first one is about Anne going to Skegness and the caravan at Ingoldmells. The second one is about the trip to Skegness fun fair. The third one is about lazing on the beach and her Mum going to bingo during the next few days of the holiday. And the fourth one is about the last day.

Each time you begin a new paragraph you should set it in about the space of five letters. (Printers use two spaces but we think five is about right for handwriting.) This is called indenting and in this paragraph the word 'Each' has been indented.

Now write out Anne's letter in four paragraphs. Oh, by the way, she has made a few mistakes in this letter. Can you correct them at the same time?

Jim is not very good at writing letters. He is getting more interested, however, because he has just read in the paper that some letters were sold in London for several thousand pounds. He reckons that in a few years' time people will be clamouring to buy the letters of Jim Smudge, the first man on Mars. He makes the same mistake as Anne and writes his letters out in one big block. We think you had better read this:

```
Northampstead 1234          66 Lemon St
                             Itchfield,
                             Northampstead,
                                Herts
                             HN32 1TS
                              12th November 1976


Dear sir
I have been trying to find your catalogue but
I seam to have lost it.  What I want is one
of your Liberator bomber kits.  I mean the
big one not the small one I am enclosing three
pounds which I think is about the price, I
will send you more if it has gone up.  My
freind and I are very keen on tanks of the
last war but their do not· seam to be meny in
the shops don't you think it would be a good
idea for you to make some.  I'm shore they
would sell.
                    Yours
                      Jim
```

We think that this letter should be in three paragraphs. But before you begin to correct it there are some other points to look at as well:

Check.   The setting-out of the address
Check.   The salutation should be written like this:
          Dear Sir (Note the capital 'S')
          If the letter is to a lady it should begin:

Dear Miss   Dear Madam or Dear Ms

Check. A business letter should end:
'Yours faithfully' (Note the small 'f')
If you are fairly friendly
'Yours sincerely'
is the best ending.

Check. What should he have put instead of 'Jim'?

Oh, there are one or two other mistakes in this letter. See if you can find them as you write out the letter in three paragraphs.

Here is an example of a correctly written business letter. It is written by Jim's Dad:

```
                        66 Lemon Street
                        Itchfield
                        Northampstead
                        Herts
                        HN32 1TS

                        Tel: Northampstead 1234


13 November 1976


Colonel A Redface
Bon Repose
Snobs Lane
Northampstead
Herts


Dear Sir

I was sorry to hear your complaint about my
son James.  You were indeed right to complain
to me about the damage he did to your hedge.
```

I was also shocked to hear of the gesture he
made when you told him off. He certainly
should not have poked his tongue out at you.

I have questioned him and it seems that he and
his friends were playing some kind of game
called 'battering rams'. So it was not really
sheer vandalism as you stated in your letter.
I have forbidden him to play this game again
and will be stopping his pocket money until
the damage is paid for.

May I repeat my regret at the inconvenience
he has caused.

I enclose a cheque for £10.00 to cover the
damage.

Yours faithfully

T. Smudge

T. Smudge.

Write down any differences you may have noticed between
this typed business letter and a good handwritten letter. You
may then like to copy it out as a model.

We have not told you everything about business letters, but
just enough for your purpose. Anne will learn more if she
takes a secretarial course at college.

N.B. Some teachers still prefer full punctuation of the addresses, the salutation and the subscription. This is correct.
What is incorrect is incomplete punctuation.

21 Mixed errors

One day Jim was off school. Next day he brought a note in from his father. Mr Wright was a bit suspicious because Manchester United had been playing the local team in a cup tie replay the previous afternoon. Can you see any reasons that made Mr Wright suspicious?

Northampstead 1234

66 Lemon Street

Itchfield

Northampstead

Herts

HN32 1 T S

21st November 1976

Dear Mr Wright

I am soRRy that my son James could not come to school yesterDay as he was getting ready for school he bought up his cornflake's. He said his throat was saw so as their are alot of bad throats about I kept him off, he is quiet alright now. I Know I should of rung up but my wife and I where very busy.

yours Faithfully

T Smudge

22 No, now and know

Both Jim and Anne mix up *no, now* and *know*.

No and *know* are mixed up by them because they are both pronounced the same. You must learn, if you make this mistake, that *know* means *knowing* or having *knowledge* of something, while *no* is the opposite to 'yes' or else the figure 'o'. Here are some examples.

The greengrocer had *no* apples.
'*No*, I am not going to do that,' said Anne.
'I *know* the answer to that,' said Jim.

Now gets mixed up with *know* because they are spelt very similarly, but they are pronounced differently. So always check these three words in your head. *Now* means 'at this moment of time'.

Do it *now*.

Be careful always to write *no one* and *nobody*. Never write *knowone* or *knowbody*.

Here is a piece of Anne's work to correct. She was asked to write a puzzling conversation.

```
        "Know you can't do that now," she said.

        "Why not?" asked Anne.

        "I don't no that I should tell you know,"
said her mother.

        "But I want to no," said Anne

        "I think know-one should no," said her
mother.
```

"Can't you tell me the reason I shouldn't no?"

"There is now reason. Or at least there is not one I can tell you know."

Anne looked at her. "I think I no," she said.

"Has your father told you?"

"No."

"Then how do you no?"

"I shan't tell you know."

"Know," said her mother, "I shouldn't, but I don't think you no really. Knowbody should no."

"Now I've got you," said Anne. "You don't know whether I no or not now."

"Now, I don't," said her mother.

You might like to continue this conversation keeping up the mystery. Or else you can write separate sentences using *no, now* and *know* in the order given:

1	no...now	6	know...know
2	no...know	7	now...no
3	no...no	8	now...know
4	know...no	9	now...now
5	know...now	10	Try and get all three in in any order

23 Here and hear

One of Jim's and Anne's main problems is those words which sound the same. *Here* is another of Jim's. This time it's *here* and *hear*. This is really one of the easiest ones to correct because *hear* has the word 'ear' in it and it is always connected with *hearing*. *Here* mainly means 'at this place' or 'at this point'. But if you remember about 'ear' in the word 'hear', you will get it right. *Here* Jim is writing a bit more seriously. 'About time too,' can I *hear* your teacher say?

"Hear they are over here," he said.

"I can't here you," she said.

"Of course you can here me."

"No I can't hear you."

"I said it's hear. Hear!" he shouted.

She put her head closer to his. The wind rose. The darkness grew worse. They were prodding their poles in the snow.

"Here, I'm sure I've found something."

She still could not here what he was saying but she guessed. Hear was the spot where the bodies were buried in the snow. She could feel him bending down, putting his ear to the hole to see if he could hear breathing. Her pole struck something. "Yes they are hear!" she shouted.

The wind was now so strong that neither could hear the other. They would have to rely on the routine they had practised hear on the mountain so many times.

Now write separate sentences using *here* and *hear* in the order given:

1 here . . . here
2 here . . . hear
3 hear . . . hear
4 hear . . . here

24 Its and it's

Like many adults Jim has trouble with *its* and *it's*. He is in good company. In the town where we live there is a notice painted outside the town hall with the wrong one. *It's* quite simple really. *It's* means *it is* or *it has* and is an abbreviation. If you don't mean one of these it must be the other word *its*. *Its* is an ownership word like 'the cat lost its fur'. Here is a letter of Jim's to correct:

Northampstead 1234   66 Lemon Street

                        Itchfield

                        Northampstead

                        Herts

                        HN32 1TS

                        10 December 1976

Dear Sir

I think it's a shame that the team has lost
it's form. I mean its not long since it was
at the top of its league. Personally I think
its the fault of the manager. I know he gave
the team it's attacking image but that's no
good with a defence like its got. I mean its
a crying shame to have the backs so far up the
field. It's no help to the goalie. Even the
pitch has lost it's true surface since he came.
Now the ball bounces all over the place as
though it's a ping-pong ball.

                    Yours faithfully
                    Jim Smudge

25 Whose and who's

Both Jim and Anne have trouble with *whose* and *who's*. It is a similar problem to *its* and *it's*. *Who's* means either *who is* or *who has* and you must always test to see if that is what you mean. *Whose* is the ownership word like 'the man *whose* temper always got him into trouble' I wonder if your teacher, *whose* patience is remarkable, is wondering *who's* going to get this right? This is a typical piece of Jim's, *whose* writing style you should all be familiar with by now. Oh, by the way, he may still be getting *it's* and *its* mixed up as well.

"Whose is this gun?" said the detective inspector, holding it up.

"I'll tell you who's it is," said Whitey on who's face was an evil grin. "Its Terry Raven's. I'm sure that's who's gun it is. And that body on the floor is Alan Flack whose Terry's greatest enemy.

"I know whose body it is," said the inspector coldly. "First we'll see who's fingerprints are on the gun."

"Just a minute!" Jim stepped forward. "It's not Terry's gun. I can tell you whose it is."

"Not Terry's gun!" shouted Whitey who's face was now twisted with anger. "Of course its Terry's gun!"

"Who's word would you rather take?" asked Jim. "Mine or a man whose been in and out of prison hundreds of times."

26 Your and you're

Again like many adults Anne does not know the difference between *your* and *you're*. (We saw this mistake in a newspaper recently.) In fact she writes *your* all the time.

You're is an abbreviation of *you are*. Test yourself by asking whether you mean *you are*. If you don't it must be the ownership word *your*.

Right then, here is *your* test of Anne's work. Now let's see if *you're* any good at it:

When your young it's not easy to know your own mind. At school your expected to know all the answers in your subjects. The teachers don't realise that your not as experienced as they are. They say that your an idiot and things like that when your not at all. Then they mark your work with comments like 'careless'. That really gets your back up. Your Mum tells you that your only young once and that you have a great time with your friends but I am not sure.

Your Dad tells you to stop moaning as it was much harder when he was a kid and your much better off than he was. But I don't think he really remembers.

27 Mixed errors

Here is a piece of work which needs correction. We are not telling you whether it is Jim's work or Anne's work. We want you to decide that when you have finished from the kinds of errors you found.

Their is an old ruin of a monastry near were I live, I quiet often like to go their and sit on the stone's and think about the monk's. I reckon thay must of had a good time in those days. Their are pools at the end of the field. Thay was used for providing fish which must of been a main source of diet. Thay was also very fond of wine and beer but thay probably had to drink that because the water was not pure. Its a bit creepy there. When the wind is in a certain direction threw the stone walls I think I can here them chanting. Its said that you can see

the ghosts of three monks walking threw the
grounds at Christmas time. Thay are surposed
to be the ghosts of the monk's who's bodies was
hacked to bits by an angry Duke. The monastry
was realy distroyed by the plague which killed
alot of monks then it was burnt down by vandals
who stole the silver ornaments. The stones was
used to build a castle for an ancestor of the
Duke.

28 Common spelling errors and tests

Some spellings Jim and Anne have got wrong from time to time

a lot	anything	busy
aeroplane	author	caught
almost	basin	ceiling
already	because	character
all right	beginning	clothes
also	believe	colour
although	beneath	coming
altogether	biscuits	couldn't
among	broken	decide
any	business	despite

describe
description
destroy
didn't
different
dining
disappear
disappoint
disease
disgusting
does
doesn't
dropped
enough
etc.
everybody
everyone
February
flies
first
friend
frightened
getting
goes
hadn't
happened
having
heard
idea
immediately
in case

in fact
interest
itself
jealous
kept
language
learnt
lightning
listened
making
many
meant
minute
necessary
neighbours
next
noise
nothing
nuisance
occasion
occasionally
old-fashioned
opinion
other
ourselves
parents
pollution
probably
professional
really
says

separate
shining
shouldn't
skeleton
sincerely
someone
something
sometimes
speech
spies
stopped
supply
supposed
surprise
their
themselves
they
tough
tried
tries
until
usually
vegetables
view
Wednesday
went
when
won't
wouldn't
wrong

aloud/allowed
bought/brought
father/farther
knew/new
lose/loose

seam/seem
shore/sure
threw/through
waist/waste
weather/whether

The three most useful spelling rules:

1 Knock off the 'e' for 'ing'.
2 'i' before 'e' except after 'c' when the sound is 'ee'.
3 English words end 'ly' not 'ley'.

Test your friend with words from the spelling list.

Remember, do not mark this book or it will spoil it for others

Test One (One letter missing)

–ny
auth–r
bas–n
cloth–s
d–scribe
diff–rent
dis–usting
Feb–uary
frighten–d

happen–d
immediat–ly
int–rest
min–te
pol–ution
pro–ably
real–y
sep–rate
skel–ton

sincer–ly
som–one
su–ply
su–posed
su–prise
themsel–es
th–y
veg–tables
Wed–esday

Test Two (Two letters missing)

a—oplane
am—g
bec—se
begi—ing
bel—ve
ben—th
bisc—ts
col—r

dis—se
d—s
d—sn't
fl—s
f—st
fr—nd
g—s
lang—ge

n—ghbours
n—sance
op—ion
sp—s
th—r
tr—s
tr—d

Test Three (Three letters missing)

a——ough
a——gether
c——acter
dis——ear
dis——oint
ne——sary
ne——bours
o——sion
o——sionally
prof——ional

Test Four (Each of the following is a clue for a word in the spelling list)

many	make up your mind	a lot
nearly	ruin	not modern
O.K.	eating	speaks
as well	butterfingers	bright
needs mending	satisfying	strong
above your head	and the rest	normally
arriving	receiving	not right
unable	brainwave	

29 Revision and other exercises

Other things you can do

1 Take one of the Home News pages of a newspaper. Find twenty words beginning with capital letters except those printed in block capitals or those at the beginning of a sentence. Say why each one has been used.

2 Take a piece of your own writing. Write it out without any full-stops or capital letters and hand it to a neighbour to correct. If you haven't a suitable piece take them out of our work on pages 1 and 55.

3 Find out how many apostrophes before an *s* we have used in this book, (**not in Jim's or Anne's work**). Then copy each owner word out together with the thing owned.

4 Write out Jim's joke on page 34 as speech dialogue and not as a play ('said Farmer Harry'—'said Farmer George').

5 Write out Anne's conversation on page 28 as a play.

6 Write out a conversation that could take place on a bus (a) as a play (b) as speech dialogue. Have at least four questions in it.

7 Look at Jim's and Anne's work on these pages 13, 18, 35, 45. See how you could divide it into paragraphs. Then copy out just the start and the ends of the paragraphs.

8 Write the Prime Minister's reply to Jim's letter on page 3.

9 Make up sentences using these words in the order given:

there ... quite   who's ... you're
their ... quiet   its ... here
there ... were   it's ... hear

there ... where	they're ... off
to ... of	they're ... of
to ... off	two ... here
quite ... hear	where ... your
quite ... here	off ... quiet
you're ... whose	were ... your
your ... quite	you're ... too

10 Write sentences using any three of the above words in any order.

11 Take any two pieces of work by Jim and any two by Anne. Criticize them for content and then improve on them by writing better pieces on the same theme.

Jim and Anne are making progress and we hope you are too. As we said at the beginning everybody makes mistakes. The thing is to know when you have made one and to correct it. Newspapers are printed in a great hurry and they make mistakes. How many errors have you spotted in a newspaper? We saw fourteen in a football report the other day.

We are not quite sure how much progress Jim and Anne are making. We had hoped to find out when we visited Mr Wright in the nursing home last week, but the doctor forbade us to mention Jim Smudge to him. Miss Madd has disappeared. It seems that when she was given her timetable for the next school year she had eight periods with Anne and four periods of drama with Jim and she has not been seen since she went to the travel agent's.

But we expect they'll both be back.